CSU Poetry Series IV

ALSO BY DAVID YOUNG

Poetry
Sweating Out the Winter
Boxcars

Criticism
Something of Great Constancy
The Heart's Forest

WORK LIGHTS

Thirty-two Prose Poems

David Young

Cleveland State University Poetry Center

Acknowledgement is gratefully made to the following periodicals in which these poems first appeared: *American Poetry Review* ("Four About Reflecting Surfaces," "Four About Death"); *Grove* ("Kohoutek"); *Madrona* ("Four About the Letter P"); *Paris Review* ("Sexual Groans," "The Poem Against the Horizon"); *Pocket Pal* ("Four About Heavy Machinery," "The Poem of the Cold"); *Poetry* ("Four About Metaphysics"); *Poetry Now* ("Four About Apples," "Four About Mummies"). Cover design after René Magritte, by Leonard Trawick.

All rights reserved. No part of this book may be used or reproduced without written permission except in the case of brief quotations in critical articles or reviews.

Copyright © 1977 by David Young
Manufactured in the
United States of America

CSU Poetry Series IV

Distributed by
NACSCORP, Inc., Oberlin, Ohio

Library of
Congress Catalog No. 77-075642

ISBN 0-914946-06-4

Chauncey Abbott Hans Sebald Beham Jacob Bronowski Italo Calvino John Donne Sir James Frazer Stuart Friebert Roberta Goldshlag Dewey Ganzel Bill Hamilton Keith Hollaman Pat Ikeda Judy Karasik Rick Kent R.D. Laing Fred Lessing Ann MacKay René Magritte W.S. Merwin Henri Michaux Vladimir Nabokov Steven Orlen Albert Pollock Vinio Rossi William Shakespeare David St. John Alberta Turner Athena Tacha Diane Vreuls David Walker Charles Wright Chloe Young

CONTENTS

The Poem Against the Horizon 1

Sexual Groans 2

Four About Reflecting Surfaces
   (My old home, said the tiger moth) 4
   (The tears roll smoothly and steadily) 5
   (Scene one: monster standing in a very heavy rain.) 6
   (I looked at the fields.) 7

Four About the Letter P
   (Ponies grazing where there's wild garlic.) 10
   (Let's say a white peony.) 11
   (Hauling a cake of ice from the ice-house) 12
   (How are the potatoes doing?) 13

Four About Heavy Machinery
   (A huge cement truck turns the corner.) 16
   (Cranes are not to be compared with trees) 17
   (To take some tutoring from pumps, I said.) 18
   (We have strong feelings about bulldozers) 19

Four About Metaphysics
   (Who can hold a fire in his hand?) 22
   (A glass of water and an onion for his supper) 23
   (To one side a thin church) 24
   ("How fortunate for Alabama," I thought.) 25

Four About Death
   (Naturally, no one has been more misrepresented.) 28
   (Rented the house next to mine.) 29
   (Peyote, no hot water, a relaxed attitude about magic) 30
   (I get your instructions in a letter.) 31

Four About Apples
   (As I raised it for the second bite) 34
   (For a long time we had never seen one.) 35
   (An apple is interviewed on television.) 36
   (The apple in the tree; the tree within the apple.) 37

Four About Mummies
   (Just one pause, in the sane and sleepy museum) 40
   (In the doctor's office, there is a chart) 41
   (Egypt's national pastime) 42
   (The body of the loved one) 43

The Poem of the Cold 44

Kohoutek 45

The Poem Against the Horizon

In a dim room above the freightyards, next to an old brass bed, an angel is taking off his wings. He winces a little as he eases the straps that run down into his chest: the beat of the wings is the beat of the heart.

Out of harness, the heart rolls over now. Panting like a wrestler. Such love, such soaring! Spokane and back. So good to come down, home to this room with the stained lace curtains and the sound of switch engines. So good to remove the wings, the love, the yoke the blood must wear as it paces, oxlike, the circle of its day . . .

He sleeps on his side in the overalls he was too tired to take off. Outside the window, rain runs and drips from the eaves. Overhead, the wind and the black sky belong to someone else.

Sexual Groans

They come in many sizes — small and faint, loud and thunderous. And it's a problem, what to do with them, they won't rise up to heaven where ears have the power of refusing to hear. You can't have them out on the streets, they're too intimate. So they get stored, wherever there's room: heating systems, file cabinets, the boxes that line the shelves of seldom-patronized shoestores. Sometimes in a bus station you see someone open the wrong luggage locker. Out come half a dozen sexual groans: heads turn, eyes widen, general embarrassment.

But this problem too is on its way to a solution. Deep in the woods there's an old mill, a ramshackle affair among great trees and cool reflections. People thought it had not been used for years, but look! The wheel, dripping, turns slowly, operating some wooden machinery inside. A single attendant dozes on the planks; occasionally he shifts a large, worn lever. This is where the secret of recycling sexual groans was discovered! The river looks so steady you could almost swear it doesn't move. But the great soaked wheel turns, slowly, majestically.

Four About Reflecting Surfaces

My old home, said the tiger-moth, that candle. Beautiful women lie in every graveyard. When we ate the ox we saved its skin to stuff with straw, sew up and stand before the plough. Crops and another feast next year, we thought. The railroad station is a good neighbor to the tracks, but the train has long since passed through, thinking ahead to the mountains, the wavering splintering trestle, the plunge into the gorge.

The tears roll smoothly and steadily down the face, they leave tracks, the tracks shine, the tears drop from the chin onto the shirt and make little dark spots and streaks. It's a great relief, this weeping. And then there is the tongue. It doesn't know baby, it doesn't know mother, it doesn't know eggs or tea or pickles. It is the tongue that licked the cool mirror, but right now the taste of those tears is the only thing it can think of.

Scene one: monster standing in a very heavy rain. Urinating. Scene two: in a large old house, several months later. The sense of order comes from chords of smell. The mutton stew, tobacco, half-tanned leather, the hearth, the musk of the chambermaid, the watery odor of stacked books. People are getting dressed for the funeral. Everyone plans to walk. Because she was so young. The master stands in his frosty bedroom — all the casements swung wide — pulling down his vest and watching his fiery features in the pier-glass.

I looked in the fields. Saw sheep, saw furrows. Looked in the woods. Saw leaves and needles, saw standing, leaning and fallen trees. Looked in the pond by the beaver dam. Saw a cloud and a trout and a swallow and a bone and a twig and a moon. And a face that was not my own.

Four About the Letter P

Ponies grazing where there's wild garlic. "Only those who have smelled the breath of cows pasturing . . ." Thirty-four electric shock treatments. Fifty comas. Dances of women while men are away fighting. Whistling. Bumblebees around the salt. Scolding. While snow billows and blows through the orchards and windbreaks of the family farm, he moves quietly through the house, smearing blood on the walls and doorposts.

Let's say a white peony. In a jar. Water. Evening and the moon rising like a great engraving. No, like the face of a sleeper. That's better. The housewife peeking out through her curtain while I ring her doorbell. We have to feed ourselves. Ants, snails. We have to move around, even if the feeling we get is of wandering through a cold cathedral where we know we will encounter the face of the sleeper we are not allowed to photograph or describe. "Julie and her mother were at this time desperate people." Hear the bells. Open your eyes. It's the face, it's just the peony. Petals dropping on the polished rosewood.

Hauling a cake of ice from the ice-house, hosing off the sawdust, shaving it to slush that is packed around the can and dasher and sprinkled with rock salt, taking turns with the crank, doing this every Sunday morning through a whole summer so that some hundred people may have ice-cream with chokecherry sauce, and never once thinking "This is a piece of the river."

How are the potatoes doing? From the field where you have come to inspect them, you can see the lights of the farmhouse not far off. Getting old, you think. Getting cold. Swear on this stone you will not steal yams. Thunder brings them to the surface. Long pigs run loose through the woods. The police can chase them. We sit on a verandah, sipping punch. "Magic," the psychiatrist says, "is contagious." Someone snorts. Soft moss, and the sound of a river. And pigeons, rosegray like the winter woods, rising up startled.

Four About Heavy Machinery

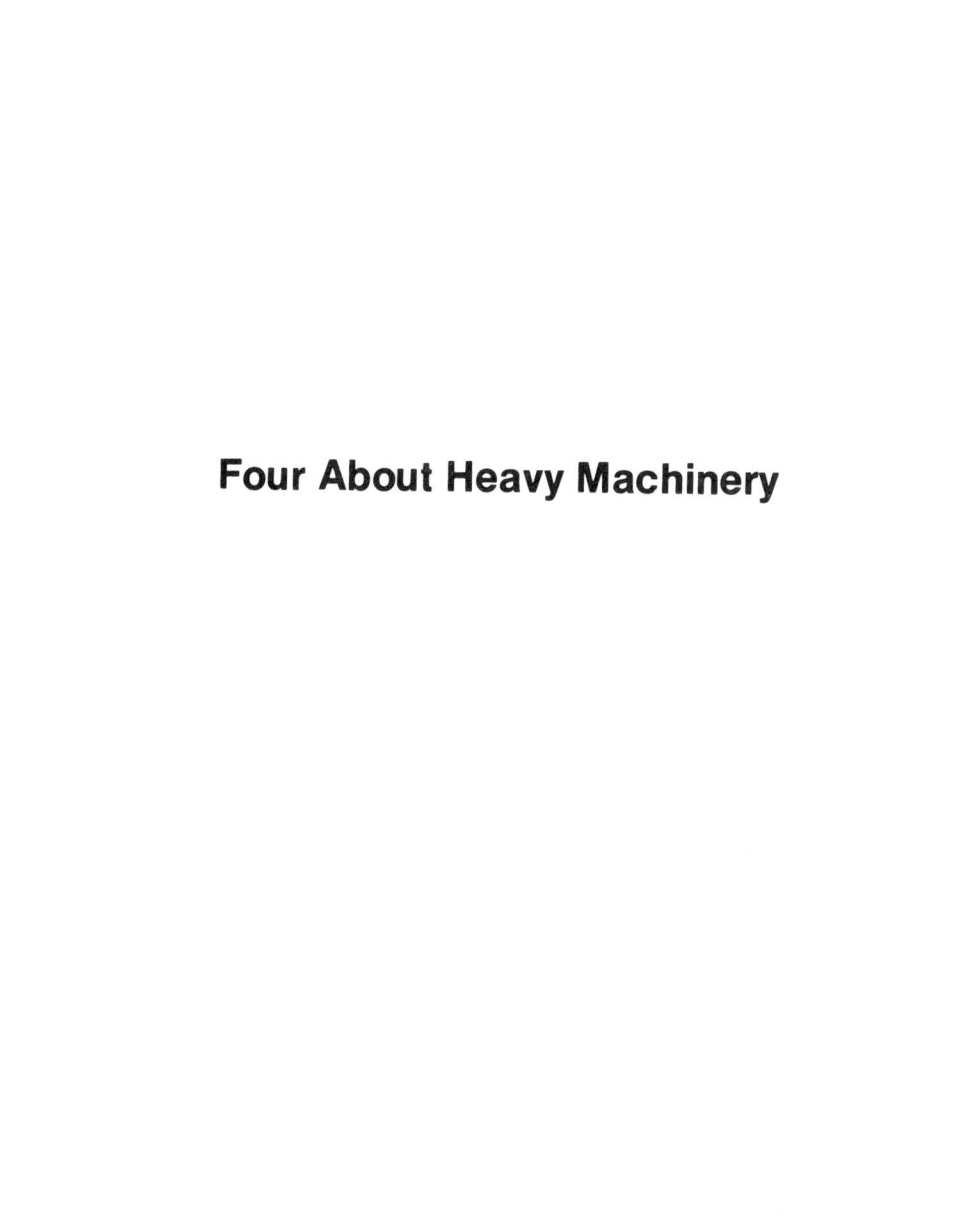

A huge cement truck turns the corner, and you get the full impact of its sensuality. Those ruts in the road or on the lawn! Even at night the cement plant has a strange energy, drawing adolescents to stare through its fences, causing the watchman to shine his light nervously among the parked and sleeping mixers. Still, from those fluid beginnings and slow revolutions, the cement itself forms the pale and stony squares of sidewalk. Reassuring. Roller skates, hopscotch, salted ice. Then the slow cracking from the tree roots below and we are back to sensuality again.

Cranes are not to be compared with trees, not with their almost Scandinavian sense of the importance of duty and power. Sometimes the face is very far from the heart, and the one thing you would like to do — lie down next to that beautiful passing stranger, for instance — is the thing that seems least possible. So you sway against the gray sky, pretending to a stiffness you do not feel. The building you helped create rises toward you, filled with the sounds of hammering and the strange shine of worklights.

To take some tutoring from pumps, I said. I was thinking about the windmill, that swaying, clanking lecturer. Slow cows come to drink from the tank. We filled it, didn't we, harvesting water from weather, not by bringing it down from the sky like rain, but up from the earth like oil. Now roll up your blue sleeve and plunge your arm into that tank. If you clench and unclench your fist regularly you can learn something about the submersible pump, beating down there where weather is a dream.

We have strong feelings about bulldozers, their buzzing and scraping, their clumsy abruptness, their way of tipping saplings into piles of burnable roots and brush. Our faces get vinegary when we think of it. But the bulldozer's point of view is remarkably different. The bulldozer thinks of itself as a lover. It considers that its loved one, from whom it is always separated, is wrapped in many short, soft, buttery strips of leather. It imagines itself removing these worn leather wrappings, one at a time and with great tenderness, to get at the body of the loved one. Perverse, you will say. But see, you have already entered the life of the bulldozer: your hands reach for the next piece of leather. Shrubs and young trees go under.

Four About Metaphysics

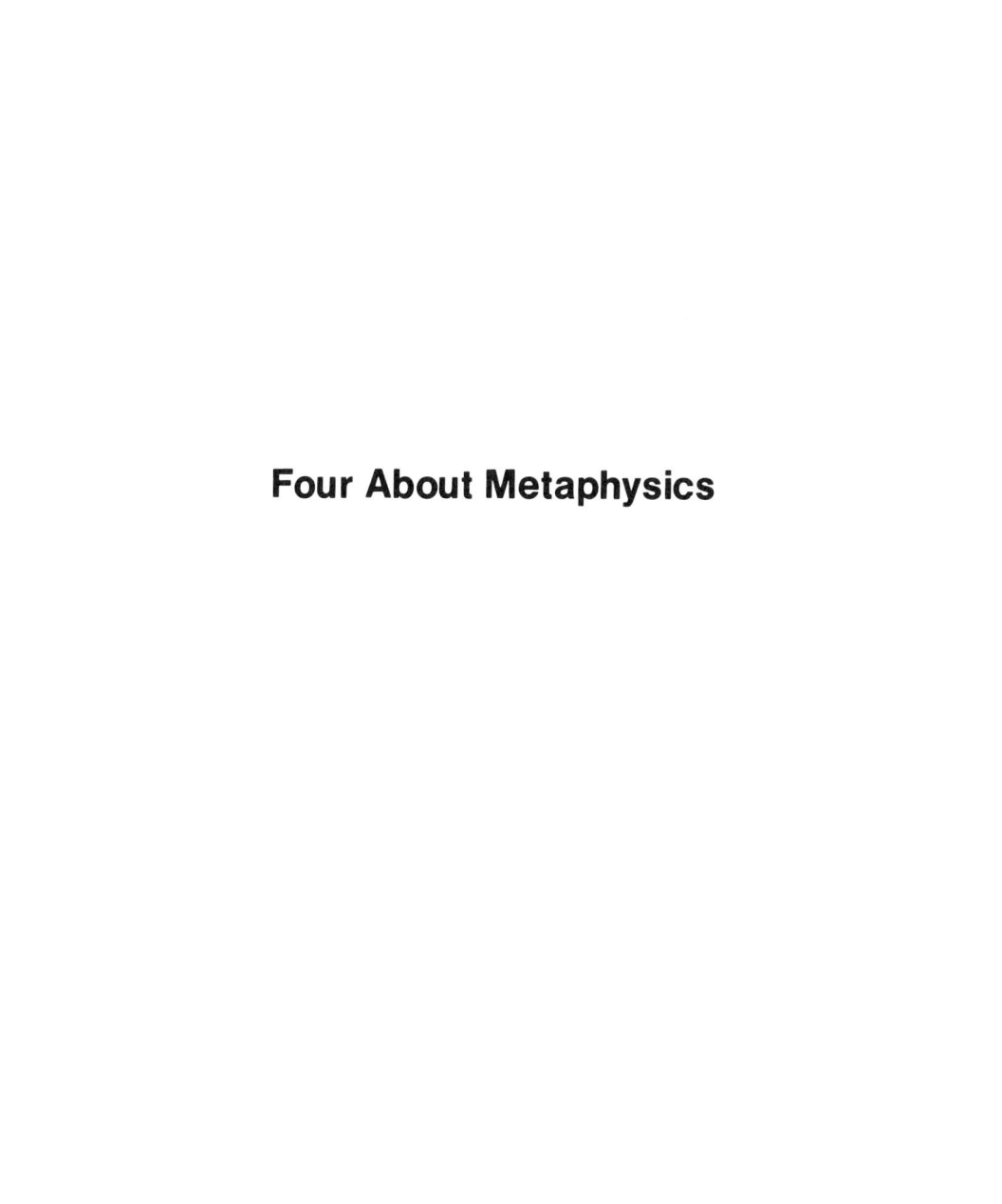

Who can hold a fire in his hand? You spread your fingers. Ideally, they should be a substance like cork, and your palm a substance like hooves. Or antlers. A stag can poke his horns right into a furnace, can't he? Even if he can't, he probably thinks he can, whereas we feel vulnerable in the presence of vast spaces, extreme conditions. That far-flung glitter through which the midget spaceship floats. Or the frosty Caucasus. Or the snapped axle of a covered wagon halfway across the desert. Or the excitement of seeing whales surface by lanternlight. All around you. In the dark Pacific. If you didn't have to consider the boat capsizing and the light going out. If you were the boat and your hand its own unquenchable lantern.

A glass of water and an onion for his supper, the Spanish visionary sat at his table in the future. Ultimate secrets were streaming from the monastery. A rowboat was crossing the very blurred lake. Sex, for him, was just an impolite kind of staring. But the blue-eyed countess did not seem to mind. Millions of things sought to claim his attention, and he tried to look beyond them. Remembering this sentence: "The sea is as deepe in a calme as in a storme."

To one side a thin church, flying a flag or a pair of pants. In the distance a castle from which a flock of rooks streams up in a spreading wedge. Someone fumbling with a barrel. And at a long table before a peeling house, people are talking, eating, fighting, kissing. Noticed by a dog, one man is vomiting. A group of musicians can be seen through the smoke from the cooking fire. About to appear from over the hill, someone like Tamburlaine or Genghis Khan.

"How fortunate for Alabama," I thought. I was turning the pages of a book that resembled a piece of ice. Rapidly, as if I feared it would melt. I passed the song, the recipe, the sermon, the code, and the questionnaire. I passed the sketch of the wrestler, flexing his muscles and sobbing. I passed the poem about shooting stars and puritan names. I was searching for the story that begins: "God was not even allowed to touch Mary. It seemed to him sometimes that if he could just take her face in his hands, the world would reassemble itself with excitement. But he did not. Meanwhile, the seed..." And so on. I could not find that story. I came instead to this.

Four About Death

Naturally, no one has been more misrepresented. The large dark eyes, for instance, with their penetrating glance. In fact, they are blind. But if you put your own up close to them, you begin to glimpse the many things within: the lovers in their squirrel cage, the panel discussion, the feast of the green-gowned goats, the bull's-eye lanterns strung through coastal villages. "So that is the sort of thing," you muse, "that lies beyond." The answer to that: not necessarily.

Rented the house next to mine. Aloof at first, seen occasionally clipping the hedge or putting out rabbit poison. Friendly waves as our carts passed in the grocery. Now and then limousines in the driveway, late lights, soft bell music. Thick red hair, golden beard, long fingers. When I realized he was spying on me, he confessed immediately, face ablaze. We discussed his loneliness and reached an understanding: weekly visit for tea and backgammon. We also exchange books, amidst disconcerting hints of greater intimacy to come. Something in that firm handshake makes me think I was wrong to take pity on him.

Peyote, no hot water, a relaxed attitude about magic — the American Indians got to know her extremely well. An Indian child could go sit with Death and chat. Such conversations tended to be dominated by her opinions. She considered the Cheyennes "autograph-seekers." She called the Aztecs a name that translates roughly as "The Heavies." About the Pawnees: "It's ridiculous, all those stories about Beaver Woman this and Buzzard Man that." As for the Navajos, she resented their interest in her relation to darkness, mosquitoes, intoxication, and travel. Her comments suggest a gruff affection. Which was reciprocated. Often. And with considerable taste.

I get your instructions in a letter. A small plane drops me at an airfield in the Andes. I stand by a rusting hangar, watching it climb out of sight. No one's around. Farther up the mountain animals I have never seen are grazing. Higher still a few clouds, resting against rocks. You do not arrive when I do. I must live in a hut for an undetermined space of time. Now and then I walk down to the village, carrying a basket for food and a jug for wine, but such things interest me less and less. Night storms light the mountains with blue flashes and send gusts of wind and rain that flatten the meadows. The morning of your arrival, I see a hare raised up, watching me. I do not know if you will come down the mountain or, more slowly, from below. All I know is that I will go out to meet you. My soul will be in my mouth.

Four About Apples

As I raised it for the second bite, I saw a tiny man, waving his arms and cursing in French. A surrealist. I looked away in embarrassment. How could I explain to him that he had mistaken my apple for a *pomme*? You know how touchy these "little masters" can be. Not to mention the language barrier, which is eight feet, three and a half inches. *"Odeur misérable de pourri!"* he screamed. *"Sot, fesse, espèce de con!"* When you need an interpreter for your apple, things have come to a pretty pass. I put it down and went to the movies.

For a long time we had never seen one. Only its map. It was hard to imagine the apple's true shape because the map was flat. Perhaps it is like a football, some said, picturing a tasty red oval sailing through the end zone. No, others insisted, more like a potato, a head, two bowls glued together, a tulip, a horse turd, that lump at the front of your throat, a cheek . . . The appearance of real apples in due course ought to have resolved the whole question. But the ways in which they did not correspond to the map were suspicious, disconcerting.

An apple is interviewed on television. It looks handsome, in a waxy way, and has a disarming air of simplicity. To the interviewer's probing questions it replies with genuine candor about its prejudices ("You can't deny tomatoes lack a core"), its hopes (reparations for Genesis), its justified pride in that ancestor who took such careful aim at Newton. But when a question reveals that the apple writes poetry, it grows curiously evasive. Asked about its father and mother, it shrugs. Asked about influences on its work, it begins to tremble. There is a strange scuffle with the interviewer, the screen goes blank, and then there are commercials for windmill kits, owl feeders, rubber gloves.

The apple in the tree; the tree within the apple. Apple of the desert, desert of the apple. The apple in the body, pulsing; the body in the apple, cursing. The tower with its high room where an apple rests on the table next to a dark green bottle. The apple with wings, escaping through the casement, soaring out over the cemetery, resting-place of flesh and seeds, the same place where, next to a freshly-dug grave, a coffin full of apples waits for burial.

Four About Mummies

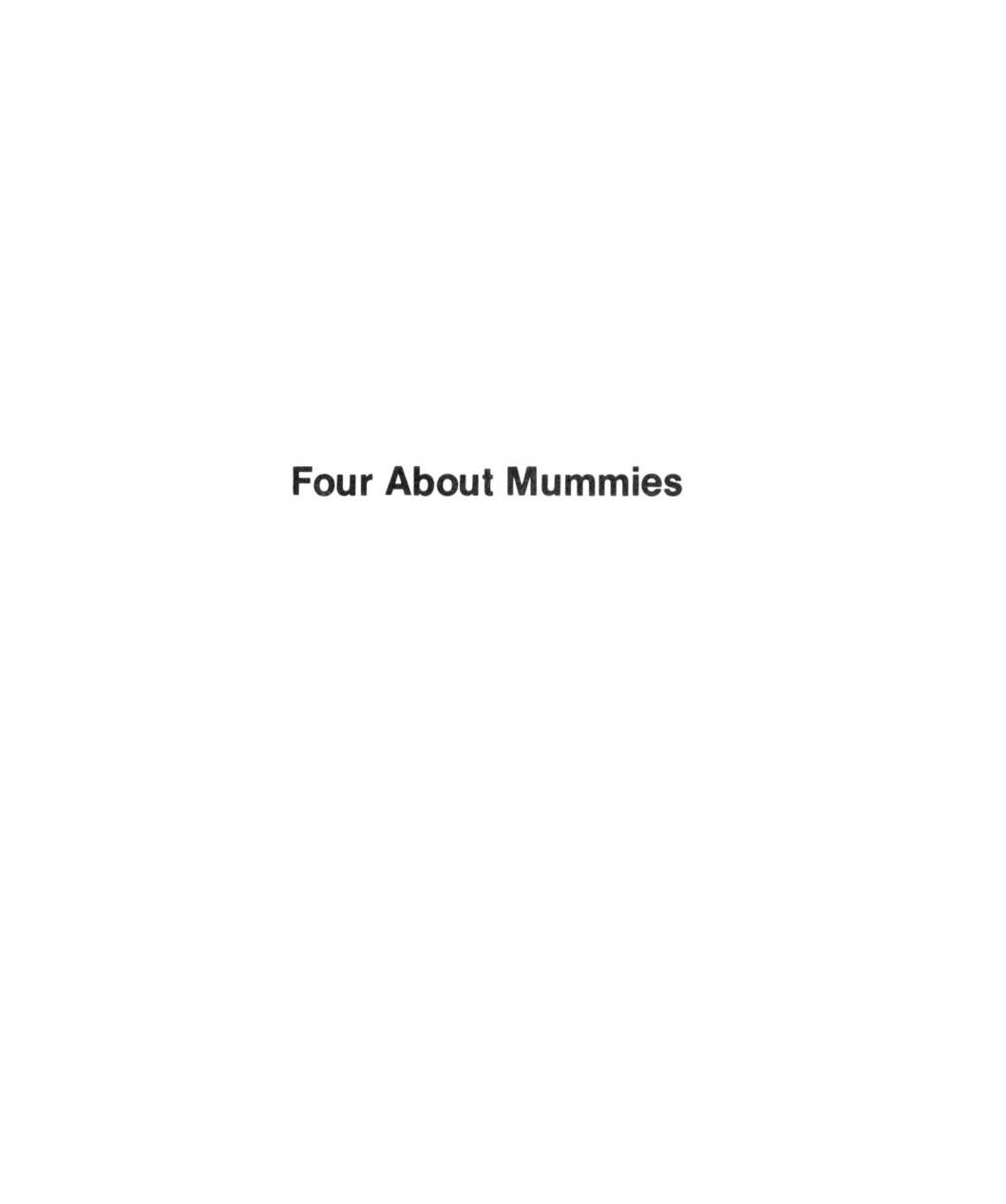

Just one pause, in the sane and sleepy museum, is enough. You see the box, with its lid askew, the bone among ancient rags, it dawns on you that the face is not a mask. Now you will be related to it all your life. It will meet you by starlight in the courtyards of sleeping cities. Dressing or undressing your body, you, will remember that box, face, rags. And in the horror movies, as you watch its caricature strangle and abduct the foolish archeologists, your smile will tighten and then vanish.

In the doctor's office there is a chart of the circulatory system. A blue and red thicket grows, but the figure it inhabits is otherwise white and blank; and the hands are spread, as if imploring. But communication is next to impossible. It is said that they have their own language, a compound of muffled odors in which they converse like birds. If you were patient and had a keen enough nose, a dark pyramid would be filled with a melancholy, spicy twittering.

Egypt's national pastime, given their history, skill, and climate. But we must not forget other nations. Some will have heard of certain North and South American Indian practices. A few may at least have an inkling of the Irish mummies, safe in their cradles of peat. But what of the Russian mummies, famous in their lifetimes as hypochondriacs? Or the Tartar mummies, poised against horizons on their petrified steeds? Nomads who follow migrations must leave even their dying behind, but the rare, accidental mummies of the Lapps somehow contrive to keep up with the reindeer, and are sometimes even seen leading the vast, milling herds across the spring-washed tundra.

The body of the loved one, yes, tears and tar, to soak it, to wrap it, removing each organ except the heart, to fill the cavity with spices, to wrap each organ carefully and return it, to swaddle, to bandage, to blur. Does any happiness exceed this? Recall the simple pleasure of draping a shawl around someone's shoulders. And then the box: the facade, the mirror that dignifies, gaily painted, a boat, a boot, a gorgeous wooden nightgown. All of it then to be stowed in the dark where even the explorer's torch cannot reach. There, in perfect silence, with the wrapped cat, the mummied hawk, the dishes of preserved food. Don't dismiss it: *only a fool or a god would shut the book of the dead.*

The Poem of the Cold

Admit you tried to make it pretty. Start again. Talk about the huge nails going in, the serene blows of the hammer. Flocks migrate at great cost, animals crawl painfully into burrows. A starving man chews on a bird's nest, cursing. It may be true that wonderful things go on — a polished haw swinging on a tree in the oxlike wind, an old woman splitting wood next to a sand-colored barn — but you must avoid these. For you are the cold's thin voice, that thickens everything else. As you sing, warm things ball up, shrivel, stiffen. Hands become mittens, heads become hoods. Shadows lose their outlines, gates lock, waterfalls hang silent as their own bad portraits. And gradually, as you shiver and wince, your poem will grind to its own slow close, like the works of a twenty-five pound clock, freezing beside the overturned dog sled, the scattered supplies, the man whose face froze around his tears and beard, the five dead huskies.

Kohoutek

In a broad field on a clear night you might stare at the sky quite uselessly, and with expanding dismay. I had the luck to encounter the comet on a gray morning when I was doing next to nothing in an upstairs room. I may have been restless and shaky, but my attention was steady as a trout. Outside, the plane trees began to stir. Then the mirror gave a small tremor. The comet was in the closet. Shaggy and silent. I glanced outside. The same pigeons were walking on the brown corrugated roof next to a skylight. But for a few fine moments, all the terrifying diffuseness — of matter, of winter light, of interest and love, of the Great Plains and the galaxies themselves — was just exactly bearable!